Grandma's Ring

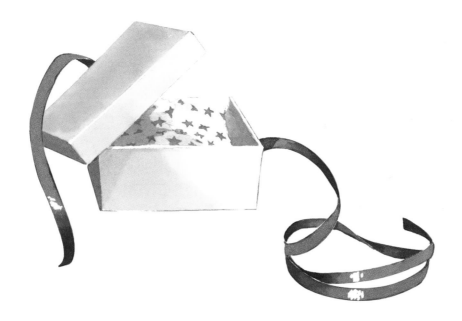

Martin Waddell
Illustrated by Denny Bond

Rigby®
A Harcourt Achieve Imprint

www.Rigby.com
1-800-531-5015

Grandma sent Rose a very special present. It was a ring that had been passed through the family for many years.

Grandma said it was a family
treasure. That's why she gave it
to Rose.

Her mother put the ring on
a red ribbon that hung around
Rose's neck. The ring was too
big to fit on Rose's finger.

"Grandma is coming to stay with us for a few days," Mom told Rose. "I think she'll be very proud to see you wearing that ring around your neck."

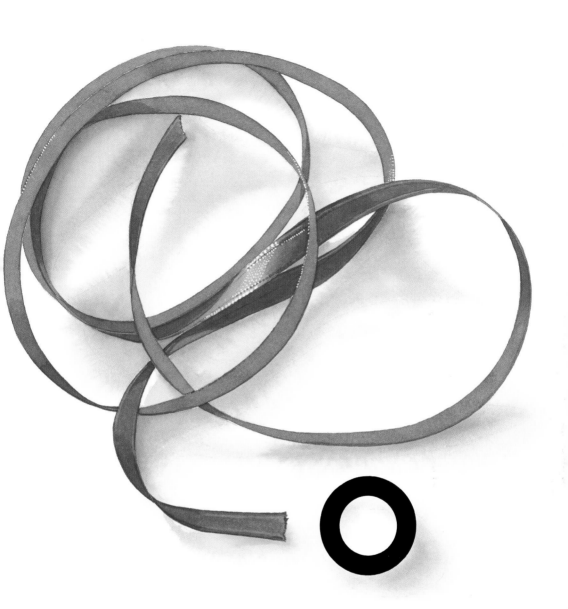

But Rose wanted to show
Grandma the ring on her hand.
She took it off the ribbon and
slid it onto her finger. It was
too big.

Later, Rose went to play in
the snow-covered fields with her
big sister Marie. Rose put the
ring on over her glove to make
it fit better.

Rose and Marie ran to the barn. They hid behind bales of hay and threw snowballs at each other.

Later, they made a snowman in the yard near their house. They gave him a carrot for a nose and put their dad's old hat on his head.

Rose had forgotten all about Grandma's ring.

"Frosty toes! Frostier nose! It's time we went in," Marie said as she shivered.

They went in to dry by the fire and watched the steam rise from their wet clothes.

Suddenly, Rose remembered the ring. She looked at her hand, but there was no gold ring.

"I've lost Grandma's ring! It must have come off while we were playing!" Rose gasped.

"You can't have lost it!" said Marie.

"But I *did* lose it!" wailed Rose. "And Grandma is coming tomorrow."

"The snow is bright white and the ring is shiny gold," Marie reminded her. "It shouldn't be too hard to find."

They searched in the barn, all
around the farm, here and there,
there and here—everywhere—but
there was no gold ring.

They searched around the
snowman, but there was no
gold ring.

"Maybe our snowman ate it,"
Rose grumbled.

"I don't think so," Marie said.
"Snowmen don't eat things."

They looked everywhere they
had played, but there was no
gold ring.

"Grandma will be so sad that I lost her ring," Rose said with tears in her eyes.

Marie had to think fast.

"Listen, Rose," Marie said, "It's the earliest snow of the season. Tomorrow will be sunnier. The snow will turn to water and disappear."

"So?" Rose sniffed tearfully. "So that's how we'll find Grandma's ring," Marie said.

"The snow will turn to water. The sun will cause a lot of it to dry up. The ring will be left behind on the ground."

The next morning, much
of the snow was gone. Rose
and Marie hunted for the ring.

"Let's find it fast, Rose.
Grandma will be here any
minute," Marie said.

They searched in the barn, all around the farm, here and there, there and here—everywhere—but there was no gold ring.

They searched by the snowman. It was only a small pile of snow with a hat on it. Soon it would be just a puddle on the ground.

Rose gave up. She picked up Dad's hat to take it back inside. Suddenly Marie gasped. "Rose, look!"

Grandma's ring was sitting
on the little pile of snow.

"You were right!" Marie
grinned. "The snowman *did* eat
Grandma's ring."

Rose grabbed the ring and
held it tightly in her hand. She
ran back home and found the
piece of ribbon that her mother
had given her.

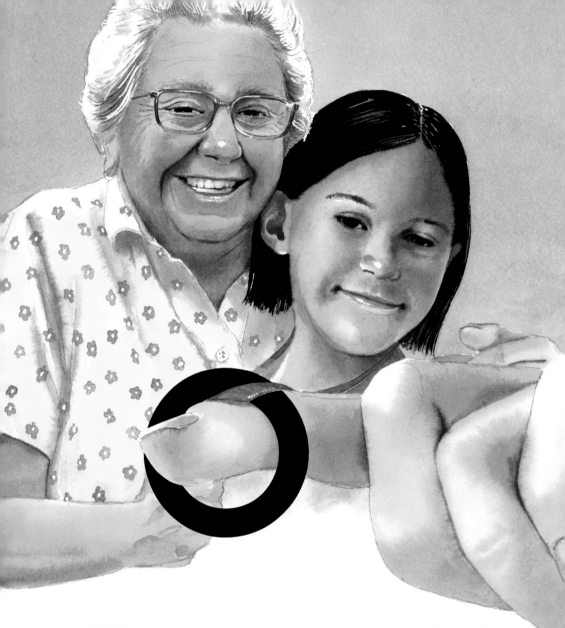

When Grandma arrived, the ring hung from Rose's neck.

"See, Grandma? I'll keep your ring on this ribbon. That way it will always be with me."